BASTIEN PIANO BASICS
SUPPLEMENTARY

INDIAN LIFE

BY JAMES BASTIEN

NEIL A. KJOS MUSIC COMPANY SAN DIEGO, CALIFORNIA

Preface

The historic customs of some North American tribes are portrayed in this book. The words with the music tell about the significance of many items and functions in tribal life. More detailed comments are given with each piece.

This book is appropriate for students in levels 1 to 3 of a piano method.

About the composer

James Bastien has written a great deal of music that has been enjoyed by both children and adults.

He has been a faculty member at Notre Dame, Tulane, and Loyola Universities, and a summer faculty member at Tanglewood and the National Music Camp at Interlochen, Michigan. When he was a student at Southern Methodist University, his piano teacher was Gyorgy Sandor.

Mr. Bastien now resides in La Jolla, California, where he and his wife continue to write music of interest to piano students.

Contents

✓ *

*To reinforce the feeling of achievement, the teacher or student may put a ✓ when the page has been mastered.

ISBN 0-8497-9321-1

The buffalo supplied everything essential to keep Indians alive: robes, caps, moccasin soles, belts, teepee covers, bedcovers, shields, arrowheads, spoons, cups, knives, soap, thread, and many other items. Because the buffalo was so important, it was worshipped as a sacred animal, and its spirit was praised before each hunt.

Buffalo Hunt!

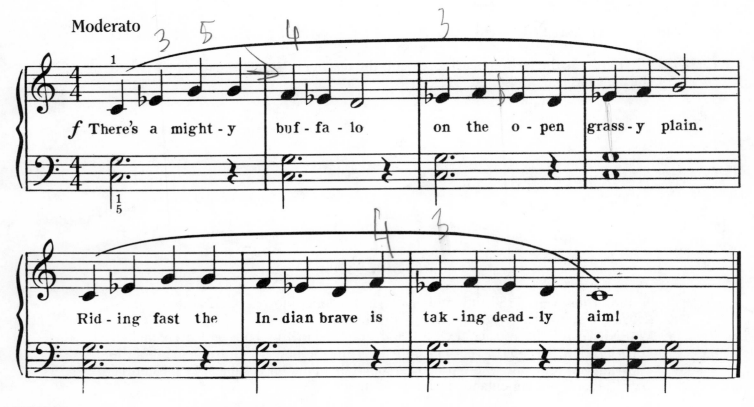

Moderato

f There's a might-y buf-fa-lo on the o-pen grass-y plain.

Rid-ing fast the In-dian brave is tak-ing dead-ly aim!

Dance for the Buffalo

With spirit

f Wear - ing shields and wav - ing spears, the In - dians sing and prance.

Wear - ing heads and wear - ing robes, they do the buf - fa - lo dance!

6

The Indian teepee provided perfect
housing. It could easily be moved as the
tribe followed the buffalo. The teepee
was made of buffalo hides which were
stitched and stretched over poles. In-
side the teepee there was room for sev-
eral beds, a fire, and firewood. Each
teepee had a front door.

My Teepee

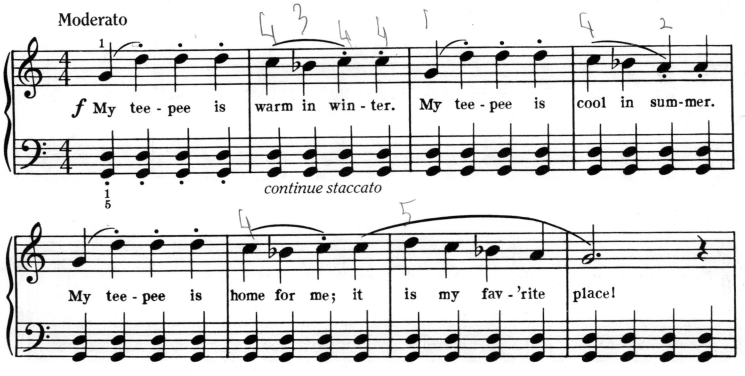

Moderato

f My tee-pee is warm in win-ter. My tee-pee is cool in sum-mer.

continue staccato

My tee-pee is home for me; it is my fav-'rite place!

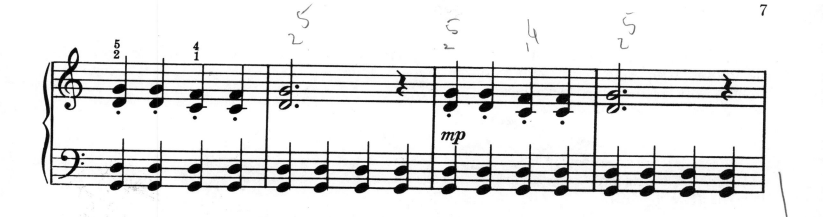

Indian baskets served many uses. They were woven from grasses, bark, yucca leaves, and other fibers. The baskets were used to store grain and seeds; some were used to store water. Some baskets took three to four month's work for the women to complete.

Beautiful Baskets

Moderato

mf Weav-ing bas-kets in the sun, will we ev-er get it done?

Yuc-ca leaves are wov-en tight. What a love-ly sight!

10

To the Indians, all things about them were filled with spirits. Spirits lived in the sun and earth, in fire and water, in rivers and mountains, and in many creatures from eagles to buffalos. The Indians performed many rituals in asking for spiritual aid.

Spirits Everywhere

The Spanish first brought horses to America in the late 17th century. Horses were found in the area that is now northern Mexico, New Mexico, and Texas. The Indians first got their horses by stealing or trading at the Spanish settlements. Later, there were wild horses that could be seized by lassoing them. The horse was an important addition to tribes which allowed them to follow the wanderings of deer and buffalo herds. Also, the horses were used by warriors in battle.

Swift Horses

With spirit

1. There's an In - dian brave rid - ing fast as light - ning.
2. He's a might - y hunt - er with bow and ar - row.

continue staccato

He is quite a sight on a horse that's gal - lop - ing!
On the plains he rides swift - ly, quick - ly does he go!

continue staccato

turn 1
under 2

turn 1
under 3

The tribal medicine man acted as a ceremonial priest. However, his main duty was to treat the sick. The medicine man had a variety of herbs and potions to drive out evil spirits. The medicine man was sometimes called upon to treat a white frontiersman's ailments.

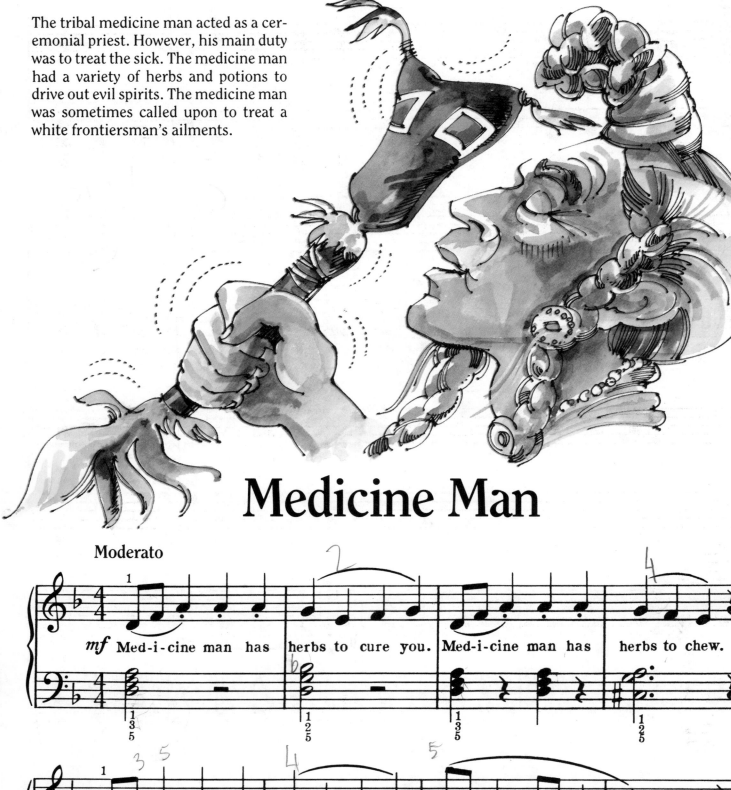

Medicine Man

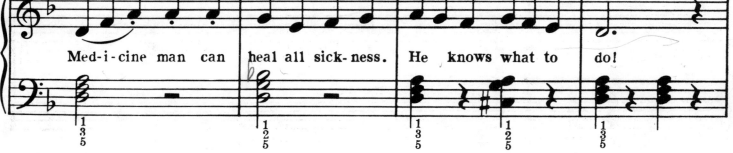

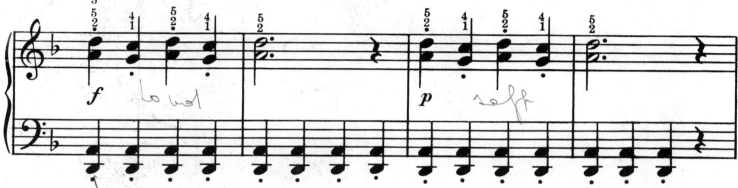

WP234

Indian children were welcomed by the tribes. Soon after birth, the mother would tie a baby in a cradleboard to be carried on her back. By the age of two or three, children were riding with their mothers on horseback. As early as five or six years, a boy might have been given his own horse. Girls of the same age began to help their mothers with cooking chores. Indian children often spent many hours listening to their elders telling stories about tribal myths and Indian lore.

Indian Children

1. In - di - an chil - dren are cute as can be.
2. Ar - rows are shot by the boys at a tree.

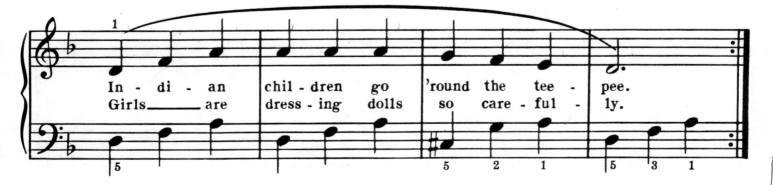

In - di - an chil - dren go 'round the tee - pee.
Girls_____ are dress - ing dolls so care - ful - ly.

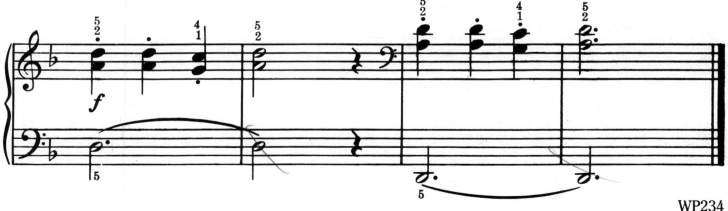

Many Indian tribes lived all across North America which now includes the United States, Canada, and Mexico. Tribes of different nations learned to speak more than their own language. In addition, sign language was another means of communication. Some of the tribes lived peaceful lives, while others were fierce warriors. Some of the major tribes were the Apache, Arapaho, Blackfoot, Cheyenne, Chickasaw, Choctaw, Commanche, Creek, Crow, Dakota, Delaware, Hopi, Kiowa, Osage, Navaho, Paiute, Pawnee, Pueblo, Seminole, Seneca, Shawnee, Shoshoni, Sioux, Uma, and Zuni.

Tribal Nations

With spirit

mf In-di-an tribes were might-y hunt-ers. In-di-an tribes were war-ri-ors.

continue staccato

In-di-an tribes form man-y na-tions. In-di-an, In-di-an tribes!

continue staccato

A birchbark canoe took months to make from carefully matched strips of bark which were laced together with rawhide. The birchbark canoe was light and graceful and easy to carry between rivers or lakes. Other styles included dugout canoes and those made of buffalo skins. A canoe was a prized possession and was often hidden under branches when not in use to avoid being stolen by other Indians.

Birchbark Canoes

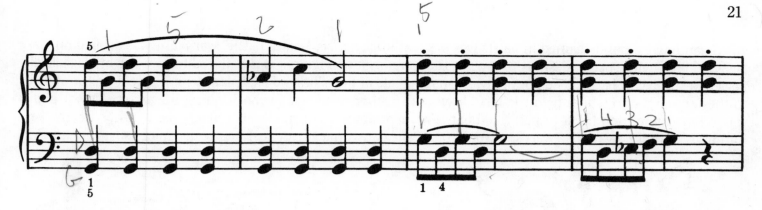

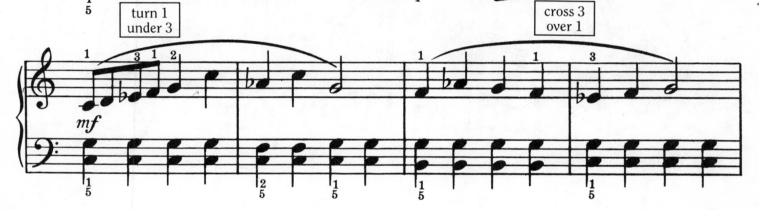

turn 1
under 3

cross 3
over 1

cross 3
over 1

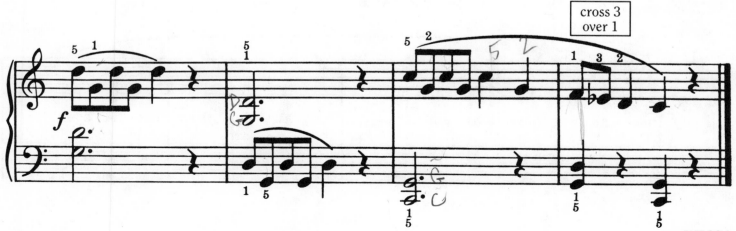

WP234

To Indian braves, honor gained in battle was of great importance. Before battle, war paint was dabbed on the face and body with special designs to protect the warrior. A war bonnet was believed to give the brave special power to survive in battle. The bonnet was usually made of bearskin and eagle feathers. A shield was strapped to the warrior's arm which held the bow, leaving the other hand free for positioning the arrows. A war club was often carried for hand-to-hand combat. Frequent raids were made on other tribes, either nearby or hundreds of miles away. The warriors would often sneak up on a village just before dawn in a surprise attack.

Indian Warriors

With spirit

mf In-di - an war-riors brave and strong, They all sing the bat - tle song.

stacc.

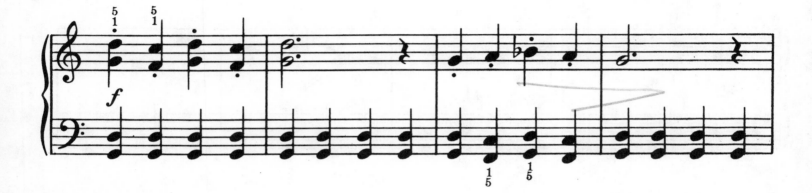

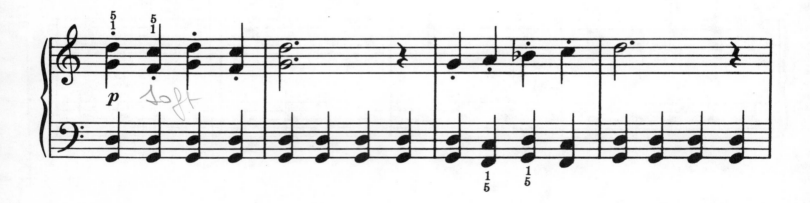